The Dedalus Press

*The Empty Quarter*

**Gerry Murphy**

GW00482793

# THE
# EMPTY
# QUARTER

## GERRY MURPHY

## DUBLIN
**DEDALUS**

The Dedalus Press
24 The Heath,
Cypress Downs,
Dublin 6W
Ireland

ISBN 1 873790 71 6(paper)
ISBN 1 873790 72 4 (bound)

**Cover painting by Catriona O'Connor**

My thanks are due to Val Bogan, Willy Kelly, Stephen Murray, Valerie Spencer and all the gang at Micromail.

Acknowledgements are made to the editors of the following publications where some of these poems were first published: *Poetry Ireland Review; Toward Harmony, A Celebration for Tony O'Malley; Innti 13; Tracks: The Snow Path*. A number were published in pamphlet form under the title **Dead Cat in Winthrop Street**, published by Three Spires Press 1994.

Dedalus Press Books are represented and distributed abroad by Password, 23 New Mount St., Manchester M4 4DE.

Printed in Ireland by Colour Books Ltd.

The Dedalus Press receives financial assistance from An Chomhairle Ealaíon, The Arts Council, Ireland.

# TEN WORDS IN IRISH

*(do Mháire Davitt)*

Í imithe
ar a Yamaha
go Omaha.

Mé buartha
buartha
buartha.

# CONTENTS

*for*
*Niamh Connolly*

# A NOTE ON THE DEMISE OF COMMUNISM

I give the Communist salute
to my Capitalist ex-girlfriend
as she takes the corner at a clip
in her black BMW,
doles me out an imperious nod
and leaves me to choke back
Marxist-Leninist rhetoric
in a plume of carbon monoxide.

# DARK TOWER  SLOW METAL SEA

Just now you passed
oblivious to my calm stare,
my unhurried heartbeat.
Even from the tower
it's easy to make out
the small disturbing swing
of your breasts,
the sudden alarming pout
of your vulva
through undulating denim.

I am in Crosshaven.
The wind is even further out
harassing the Azores.
Thinking of you
I begin to imagine
the slow honeyed burn of your skin
against
the slow honeyed burn of mine.
All this time you are in Midleton.
So much for foreplay.

Later it happens:
I am standing at the bar
quietly supping
when you pass so close
you hook your left breast
into the crook of my elbow
making me snort
into my pint.

Slipping out of my jackboots
so as not to disturb
the budgerigar
I creep softly past
the leopard's cage
only to confront
your wide-eyed
owl-awake mother.

So, I am waiting
at the bottom of the cliff path
directly below the tower
for the moon to come out
and set the slow metal sea
bristling with silver.
Afterwards, I will climb up alone.
Already my tongue
is working urgently
against the roof of my mouth
perfecting those wet flickering circles
around your nipples.

# LITTLE ISLAND REVERIE

*(for Tom McCarthy)*

Day dreaming here
where the Lee sweeps round
Blackrock castle and surges
across the sullen mud flats
towards a calm preoccupied sea.
Shore birds wheel and flash
skimming the brightening waters
in precise split-second formations,
their small piping cries
exquisitely desolate.
A freighter throbs upriver
navigation lights feeble
in the afternoon glare.
Tuan Jim, in silhouette,
brooding on the prow.

# AIMLESS IN ANDALUSIA

Arriving in Malaga
I allow the taxi driver
to talk me into heading directly to Granada
leaving the wretched coast
to my snugly packaged companions
complaining of rising green fees
and plagues of jackflipflopped Germans.

Coffee in the Plaza Nueva :
the woman at the next table
has the deep dark eyes of a matador
the glossy red lips of death.
She shakes the henna-rich cape of her hair
at no one in particular.
Nevertheless I shift uneasily in my chair
one hoof scuffing the smooth slabs beneath.

Washington Irving has it
that during his stay in the Alhambra
a favourite amusement of the peasantry
was to sit at dusk
with a long pole dangling over the battlements
and using flies for bait,
fish for birds.

Moonlight full tilt on the Generalife
glinting on helm and lance.
The murmuring of a thousand fountains
drowning the sounds of the prancing horde.
The flag of the Prophet fluttering again
from the Torre de la Vela :
Boabdil nightly repossessing his realm.

Fuente Vaqueros:
amidst the tall drowsing poplars of the Vega
behind the throbbing all-night disco bars –
the birthplace of Garcia Lorca.
Amongst the bric-à-brac
lovingly tended, gleaming with legend:
a photograph of Leonard Cohen
solemnly rocking the poet's cradle.

In Seville
I sleep out under the stars
to escape a snoring companion
who mimics the sinking and raising
of the Titanic.
Actually, I sleep on the balcony
which affords me
one rectangular strip of mauve sky,
two flickering stars
and a silvery imminence of moonlight
in a pear tree.

In the Cathedral
bent double with monument fatigue
(one more fourteenth century holy water font
and I'll piss in it)
I linger uncomprehendingly at the notice board
until comprehension dawns blindingly
with a huge photocopy of the Cathedral's entry
in the Guinness Book of Records.

After the bullying heat of Seville
Cordoba feels almost like home
at least looking to the South
and those familiar rolling hills.
This is to say nothing
of the glory of the Mezquita,
the gloomy splendour of the Alcazar de los Reyes
or the gilded sweep of the Guadalquivir.
This is to ignore
the increasingly strident graffiti:
Death to the Governor!
Death to the Prime Minister!
Death to the King!

Sorry Cervantes,
I tried to find the Posada del Porto
in which you are reputed to have stayed
after your sojourn
with the Inquisition
in Seville, but my sore feet
(my complaining Sancho Panzas)
prevailed over my worn thin curiosity.

Banality in the afternoon:
Where to now Ernesto?
Channel 3 is showing The Muppets
Channel 2 has Love of Ward Eleven
while Channel 1 is following the action
live from the Plaza de Toros in Saragossa
with instant replays, assessments and analysis,
and interviews with the matadors
if and when they dispatch their bulls.

Wait! What's this?
Kermit the Frog has just exposed himself
to Miss Piggy!

Malaga,
back to the future:
BOOZED BRITS BURN DOWN DAYGO DISCO
KRAZY KRAUTS KILLED OUR KEVIN
FROGS FLOP IN SEX STUDY
more ketchup stains
on my well thumbed Lorca,
I have taken to MacDonalds again.

## HOLY WEEK IN GRANADA

Preposterous cocktails and cocaine dreams,
paedophile covens and piss freaks,
not so much as a millisecond
of your agony shared

jesus.

## THAT FABLED SUMMER

My father
with Garcia Lorca eyes
cheerful in the garden
trimming the hedge.
The sun always fixed
in a searing blue sky,
the Falange forever gliding up
in a long black limousined hush
to the front gate.

## MY DEAD FATHER
## READING OVER MY SHOULDER

Madrid. Late November.
Mid-morning on the Plaza Cibeles
under a newly installed tinted blue
plate glass sky.
Coffee, croissants and the Herald Tribune,
simple empire of the moment.
The café's one-eyed cat
quiet amongst the pigeons
as frantic shoals of traffic
anxiously negotiate the Square.

Light on the Paseo del Prado,
light on the page
as I drowsily scan a report
of the World Series:
"first base", "pinch hit", "home run"
phrases floating out past me
as if being read by another

buy your own paper, father.

## MY MOTHER
## ALIVE AND WELL AND LIVING IN...

Six months after
the report of your death
I start a rumour amongst my schoolmates
that you are still alive.
That you are hiding out
in the Bolivian Andes
with a Lt. Colonel of the Treasury Brigade
who fled La Paz during one of three
October *coups d'état*
with thirty million U.S. dollars
and four lorry loads of gold.

Just wait for the letters
with the postal orders
I tell them.

## EPITAPH FOR AN OLD I.R.A. MAN

That gaspipe baluba, my grandfather,
has blown his last dart
into the stratosphere.
We found him grinning
under the wheels
of the Royal Carriage this morning,
his unexploded corgi-bomb
pressed to a jelly.

# MRS THATCHER'S NIGHTMARE

In the South Atlantic,
naked in a bath tub,
looking up at the Belgrano

all late hands on deck
looking down.

## POST COLONIAL AWAKENING

Pith-helmeted little imperialists
snug in the school cinema
as we watched
that pompous colonial epic
"Sanders of the River".
We shouldered the White Man's burden
gravely resolved to improve
the savage African's savage lot;
until the projectionist, Brother Keating,
ran the entire film again in reverse
dissolving our grim determination
in tears of laughter.

# MEMORIES OF OLD MOSCOW

*(for Paul Durcan)*

Spring it is:
daffodils
and leaping squirrels
in leafing trees,
the Politburo winding up
to speak
of Lenin.

# WHITE NIGHTS ON DOUGLAS STREET

### *(i)  Kind Of Blue*

Not that it means anything,
that kiss,
it was tucked away
in the steaming archives of desire
even before I turned back
into the room to exhume
the long dead party.
Not that it means anything,
the hiss of your bicycle tyres
on the wet tarmac
echoing through my head
long after you turned down
the hill and well into
Ian Dury's thumping rendition of
"Wake up and make love with me............"


### *(ii)  A Couple Of Nights Later*

A couple of nights later
I am turning over
into another dream wilderness
when a tiny residue of your scent
trapped in some hitherto undisturbed pore
is released into the still air
of the bedroom

greening the wilderness.

*(iii)  The Pleasures of Celibacy*

On Capwell Road this summer
the back gate to the church
is firmly locked.
They must have gotten wind
of those winter evenings
we spent in meltdown
against the presbytery wall.
While, in the bedroom above,
caught up in the pant
of our endless foreplay,
the young curate
prayed feverishly,
his vows creaking and groaning.


*(iv)  The Deepest Mirth*

That you may often be thus, without torment
and seldom, if ever, count sheep.
Articulating the gift of the moment
a lovely woman laughing in her sleep.

*(v)  Summer Nights  South Channel*

On Parliament Bridge
we would talk and talk
over the churning roar of water,
the occasional sigh of traffic
until the tide turned
swelling darkly in the channel,
kissing up under the arch;
making the weir shut up.


*(vi)  Dream Talk*

Too much salami
you whisper
turning into my arms.
Beware of frog swallowers
I reply
my tongue sliding down
to arouse
your drowsy clitoris.

## (vii) *Goodnight Louis Stewart*

Not thinking of you, not exactly,
down by the river actually
adding a steaming golden trickle
to its steady brown flow.
Any minute now
you will probably roar past here
hotly pursued by the harbour police.
Not thinking of you, not at all,
sitting at the window actually
entering the microcosm
by staring hard at an orange.
Any minute now
you are going to emerge
from a rip in the tablecloth
momentarily serene.
Not thinking of you, not anymore,
laid back on the bed actually
listening to Louis Stewart's liquid guitar
floating up from the kitchen.
Any minute now
he's going to play
"There will never be another you..."

# LANDSCAPE WITH AUBURN HAIR

Like a flame
your auburn hair
lights the picture
the sky expands blue to the edge
where startling white
the lighthouse rears
from a glittering sea.

## 32 FISH

*(for Nessa)*

Night settles in
along the river.
Moonlight scans
the calm blueblack flood
from bank to silvered bank.
A swan turns majestically
like a screwdriver.

## HAIKU FOR A DEAD CAT

Through the street window
a dead fish glares steadily
at my catburger.

# EXISTENTIAL CAFÉ

*(for Tony O'Connor)*

"Essence before existence"
declared the waitress
throwing a handful of flour
and a few raisins
onto the table.

"I ordered two scones"
said Jean-Paul.

# CAFÉ PARADISO

Grim armies marching
in the empty pit of my stomach
as I wait amongst the staring,
sniggering tables until
all complaints at your
increasing lateness are lost
in a sudden blur of kisses
with the waitress.

# WARM AIR FRONT

*(For Katherine)*

## *(i) Stopping the Planet in St. Luke's*

I have just come to rest
in Fruit and Vegetables
after a dizzy whirl
through Sweets and Biscuits
when you arrive in the shop
trailing bright fragrant weather,
flashing that bone-melting grin.

The Earth is momentarily still;
then resumes its slow majestic spin.


## *(ii) Breathless in the Hibernian Bar*

A tongue of flame
licks into place
above your head
as you begin to speak
and I am suddenly afloat
in the upper air
of an overwhelming inspiration.

Far below
in the absolute stillness of the bar
your one good lung
breathes for us both.

*(iii) Drowning on Wellington Road*

Not so much
singing in the rain
as charmed out of its dismal reach
by that kiss at the corner
just moments ago.
It may have put a significant dent
in that sullen mass of liquid
swirling in from the coast.

No matter,
I was already underwater
and your kiss simply snatched
that last gasp of air
I was carefully saving for it.

# FREEDOM OF THE CITY

You know thursdays and me
warp nine through the gamma quadrant
to flush dead pigeons from the shuttle bay
a slow swing around orion to collect
my twenty nine senses early morning banter
with the milkman the paper boy the post
person farsud zwingli vabblesap
beam down to the uptown grill suck on
burger chips beans sausages mushrooms
and onions tilt full fat face towards
that rare shaft of sunlight glinting off
a wing mirror dream of holding mary
mahony squeezing niamh connolly kissing
maura o'keeffe somewhere over the rainbow
somewhere over the rainbow my bollocks.

"Live long and prosper"
zzzzzzzzzzzzzzzzzzzzzzzzzzzzzzzzzzzzzzzzzzzzap.

## BLACK SCARF   BLUE REFLECTIONS

I can't remember what I was looking at
so intently that particular day probably
the cracks in the pavement or those cute
smears of dogshit which I am convinced
will eventually conform to some quasi-mystical
pattern I have already laid down in
my subconscious and lead to momentary
if ultimately meaningless revelation but
that's another story however I was aware
of that black scarf floating in and out
of my peripheral vision like a remnant
of the last anarchist banner from the last
burning barricade but then I started
looking at you I mean really looking
at you head up straight between
those beautiful blue eyes only to see
the enormous sullen bulk of myself
looking back in grim stereo.

# NOTHING HAPPENING

*(for Tony Sheehan)*

Outside the back bedroom window:
a deserted cul de sac
with a lock-up garage,
a peeling NO PARKING sign
and two leafy sycamores
warming to their allotted hour
of afternoon light angled
through a maze of rooftops.

Nothing happening:
a few chip wrappers giddy
in a sudden spiralling wind,
a paper cup spinning on its axis
and the occasional creak of the garage gate
swinging open to reveal
a gleaming red Ferrari.

## BANG

Finally sold out,
exhausted but happy,
the balloon seller
leans for a breather
on the roof
of the car bomb.

## WHAT?

I am up close to the radio,
listening late and at low volume
to the World Service
when the house shudders.
My brother is tumbling purposefully
down the stairs.
Eighteen stones of spluttering indignation
in a tiny red underpants
bearing a message from his wife:
"Would you ever go to bed,
you're keeping the canary awake . . ."

## WAS THAT SINEAD O'CONNOR?

You must have mistaken me
for someone else
which would explain
why you smiled and said hello
and why I felt as if
I had slammed into a stone wall
or that you had cut
your exact shape
through my quivering mass
like a laser through blubber.

## LETTERS TO MICHAELA

Dearest M,
I am waiting up tonight
until the city quietens,
the sea stills –
and the freaks calm down;
until the Swedish North Atlantic Fleet
squeezes eagerly out of the Baltic
and I can hear all the way from Malmö
the sound of your even-breathing
untroubled sleep.
I would send
a kiss to your eyelids
a kiss to your nipples
a kiss to your lips
but just now
you are probably spending
your Social Security money
on ice cream in Greece.

If it was raining
a sudden downpour
which made the Square swim
the taxis dive for cover
the very statues
gasp for breath –
the sound
would invariably cover
the sound of your bare feet
on the stairs;
if you were here.

There are waterholes in the Sudan
which would be big enough
to take both of us,
which would enable us to spend
the hot afternoons
immersed and undressing,
which would inevitably bring us closer together:
your eyes reflecting
smooth green desert,
your breasts finding perfect level
against my chin.

Nothing to report really:
a hint of Summer
wafting up from the waterfront,
two oranges glowing
on the bedside table,
muted traffic noise,
dreary racket-ball,
dust, fumes, the smell of Bergasol.
Nightly, under a gleaming indifferent moon
the hushed coast of the Levant
yearns for you,
especially Jaffa
whose lights through the window
beyond the abyss at the bottom of the bed,
wink longingly.

# THE EMPTY QUARTER

*(for M.M.)*

Where you are tonight
or what you are doing
is immaterial.
In this
your tent is already pitched
at a cool caravanserai
under creaking date-palms.
Your camels are watered, fed, rested
and reciting the secret names of Allah.
You are reclining
in black diaphanous silks
on a jewel encrusted divan
where I (in Richard Gere's body)
am kissing you
into a long hot shivering fit.

## PURE NAKED IDYLL

Before the afterplay
the heart lies charmed
the head forgets politics
snug between the drowsy lift
of your breasts as if
nothing in the world
could stir
breathe
sink
swim
spin.

# A MANTRA FOR MAURA O'KEEFFE

At the centre:
an ink black pool of forgetfulness
girded by trees
leaves falling into

## STILL LIFE WITH MINEFIELD

Between
what I would like to say and
what I can say
there is a small path
which you keep
under twenty four hour guard,
heavily mined and blazing with searchlights.
If I planned it carefully
I could send a note across
with news of my lovelorn lot.
Give it a second read
before you have it shot.


Sometimes
when you are wrapped darkly in yourself
I have tried approaching
the edge of your bristling discontent
to ask (as a friend would)
if you need any help
in dismantling the huge gloomy edifice
you have built around your grim humour.

I am always prepared
for you biting my head off cleanly –
but you never do
you simply chew it slowly
and spit it out
piece by piece.

A few weeks pass
and I begin to think
I have it cracked.
It's easy: breathing out, breathing in.
The obsession becomes smooth,
round and familiar.
Then you return
unannounced from Argentina,
kiss me fiercely on the navel
and with what amounts
to a casual gesture with a carving knife,
cut out one of my three remaining hearts
and eat it.


I was up early today
ready to make a deal
on the minefield
if not the actual missile-sites
but you were nowhere to be found.
I could have approached the guards

on the outer perimeter
but not being sure
of how much they knew
and being rather wary
of how they might react
to an uncertain inquiry
I thought better of it.

That little nick
you gave me
with the carving knife
is showing up well
in this ultra-violet glare
and though the bleeding has stopped
the pain lingers delightfully.

Are you making someone a present
of my drinking arm?

# KEEPING IN SHAPE

*(for Liam O'Callaghan)*

"Room for two more?"
I wheeze at the gravedigger
as we jog heavily
past the graveyard.

"Two and more"
he replies
loudly, heartily, eternally.

## THE CALL OF DUTY

"No more buggery",
whispered
the weary soldiery.

"Now, now"
said the Sergeant
"now, now".

# AN IDIOT'S GUIDE
## TO THE AMERICAN CIVIL WAR

*(for Val Bogan)*

*The Opponents Square Up*

"Any people anywhere being inclined
　　and having the power have the right
　　to rise up and shake off the existing government
　　and form a new one that suits them better.
　　This is a most valuable, a most sacred right...."

– Abraham Lincoln  1845

"It is known to senators who have
　　served with me here, that I have
　　for many years advocated, as an essential
　　attribute of State sovereignty, the right
　　of a State to secede from the Union..."

- Jefferson Davis 1860

*Fort Sumter Begins to Fester*

On the evening of December 26th 1860
Major Robert Anderson
moved his command
with admirable stealth and skill
from Fort Moultrie to Fort Sumter
thereby destroying an understanding
between the seceding States and Washington.

Did this "one true man"
make war inevitable ?


*Senator Chestnut Boasts*

In February 1861
at a gala ball in Richmond,
in an effort to impress his listeners,
Senator James Chestnut offers to drink
all the blood spilt over the issue of secession.

In April 1974
up to his waist
in the bright arterial flow of Second Manassas,
his champagne glass stained and brittle
with constant use,
he belches blood in the face
of an over-inquisitive history student
from Tokyo.

*The Birth of "Stonewall Jackson"*

On Henry House Hill,
after fighting through the morning,
the Confederates began falling back at noon
just as Jackson brought his fresh troops
into line behind the crest.
General Bee, trying to rally
his broken brigade
pointed to Jackson's men and shouted:
"There's Jackson standing like a stone wall,
rally behind the Virginians!"

or did he?
some observers claim Bee's remarks
were uttered in exasperation:
"Look at Jackson standing there
like a damned stone wall!"


*Shiloh Hits an Artery*

The twenty thousand casualties
at Shiloh
were nearly double the number
of casualties at First Manassas,
Wilson's Creek, Fort Donelson and Pea Ridge

combined.

*Antietam Goes with the Flow*

More than twice as many Americans
lost their lives in one day of battle
at Antietam as fell in combat
in the War of 1812, the Mexican War
and the Spanish American War

combined.


*Marye's Heights – The Dead Burying the Dead*

"They sprawled in every conceivable position,
some on their backs with gaping jaws,
some with eyes as large as walnuts,
protruding with glassy stare,
some doubled up like a contortionist.
Here lay one without a head,
there one without legs, yonder
a head and legs without a trunk;
everywhere horrible expressions,
fear, rage, agony, madness, torture;
lying in pools of blood, lying with heads
half buried in mud, with fragments
of shell sticking in oozing brain,
with bullet holes all over the puffed limbs."

*On the Eve of Chancellorsville*
*Jackson Dips Into the Continuum*

Stuart has just informed
General Lee and me
that Hooker's right flank
is "in the air" three miles west
of Chancellorsville.
If we can plot a route
through the wilderness tonight,
we will teach "those people"
another hard lesson tomorrow.
Keep hearing Frank Sinatra
singing "Old Devil Moon"
over and over in my head.

Who is Frank Sinatra ?


*Grant Takes the Arithmetic*

All that Summer
from Spotsylvania through Cold Harbour
to Petersburg
the butcher's bill comes due.
Wave upon wave
breasting the earthworks
and breaking in blood

on the Confederacy's prolonged death throes.
Grant wades on grimly
towards Richmond.

"I am in blood stepped in so deep..."


*Lincoln Gets His*

A half muffled explosion,
bluish smoke in the Presidential box.
"Sic Semper Tyrannis!"
or "Revenge for the South!"
or "The South shall be Free!"

whatever,
Lincoln sits sprawled
in his rocker
as if asleep.


*Davis Becomes President*

After two years in Fort Munroe,
shackled and abused,
Davis was released on bail.
He spent some months in Europe
as persistent attempts were made
to bring him to trial, conviction
and a "sour apple tree".

Returning to the United States
late in 1869
with all legal proceedings against him quashed,
he accepted the position of President
of the Carolina Life Insurance Company.


*Jim Crow's One Hundred And One Years*

"I think your race suffer greatly,
    many of them by living among us,
    while ours suffer from your presence".

                                    – Abraham Lincoln 1862


"What's the use of being free
    if you don't own enough land
    to be buried in."

                                    – Freedman (anon) 1865


"There comes a time when people get tired.
    We are here this evening to say to those
    who have mistreated us for so long
    that we are tired – tired of being segregated
    and humiliated, tired of being kicked about
    by the brutal feet of the oppressor."

                                    – Martin Luther King 1954

# SELF-PORTRAIT AT 33

Quick scan of the horizon
this "year of miracles"
reveals smouldering ruins
gradually reducing to ash,
a couple of lepers complaining
to the Department of Social Welfare
and the Department of Health,
Lazarus still cold, still flat;
nothing to get nailed up about, yet.

# FOR PEACE COMES DROPPING SLOW

*(after W.B. Yeats)*

A girl passes
on the footpath,
a girl
with a lovely brown speck
in one of her blue blue eyes
and you think
the World will probably end
sweetly after all,
or, at least
that the Bomb
will drop softly
like a Cathedral . . .

## THE END OF THE END

So that's it:
a slight tiff,
a surgical nuclear strike
in the Sea of Azov,
final conflagration.
There's no one left
to read this except Banquo
and he's just inquisitive

fuck off Banquo.

# A SMALL MATTER OF TRANSMIGRATION

*(for Siabhra)*

It's December,
there's a butterfly
in the bathroom.

It's Lenin.